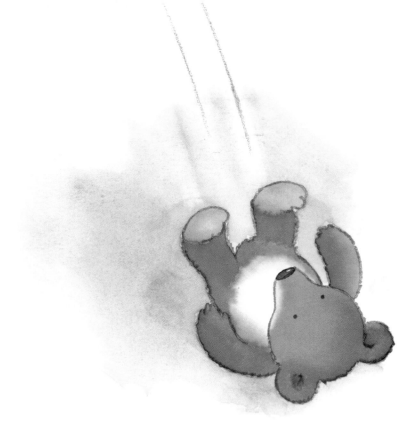

Bear
Mick Inkpen

Hodder Children's Books

A division of Hodder Headline plc

A small whooshing sound.
Then a plop!
A bounce.
And a kind of squeak.
That was how the bear landed
in my baby sister's playpen.

Have you ever had a bear fall out of the sky, right in front of you? At first I thought he was a teddy bear. He just lay there, crumpled on the quilt.

Then he got up and took Sophie's drink. And her biscuit. That's when I knew he was real.

The bear climbed out of the playpen
and looked at me.

He rolled on his back, lifted his
paws and growled.
He seemed to
want to play.

I put him in
Sophie's baby bouncer.
He was very good at bouncing,
much better than Sophie.

I sneaked the bear into the house under the quilt. At bedtime I hid him among my toys.

'Don't you say anything Sophie!' I said. 'I want to keep this bear.'

Sophie doesn't say much anyway. She isn't even two yet.

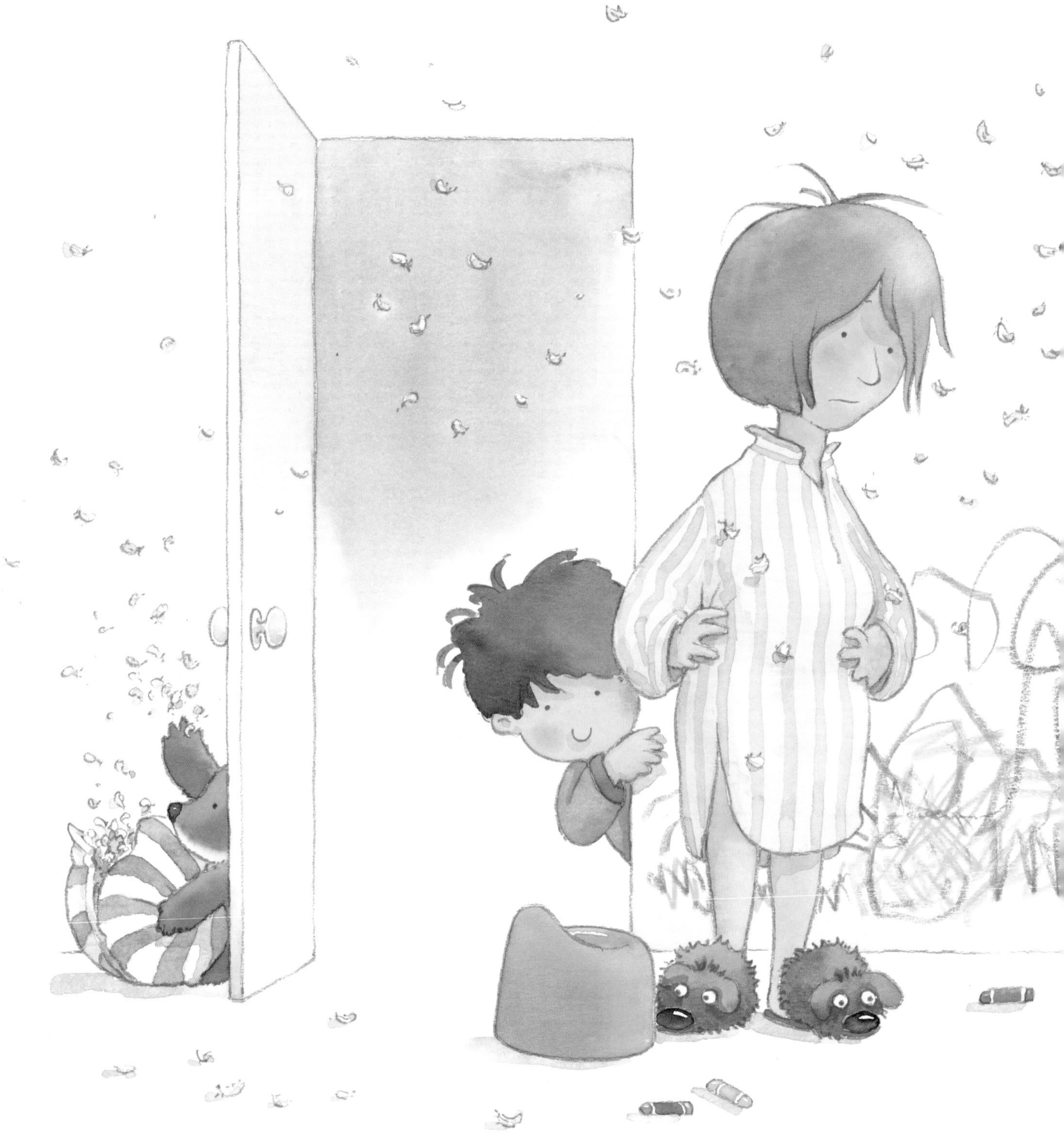

In the morning the sound of shouting woke me up.

'Sophie, that's naughty!' It was mum.
She was looking at the feathers.

'Sophie! That's very naughty!'
She was looking at the scribble.

Then she looked at the potty.

'Sophie!' she said. 'Good girl!'

But I don't think it
was Sophie.

I'm sure it wasn't Sophie.

It definitely wasn't
Sophie.

I took the bear to
school in my rucksack.
Everyone wanted to be
my friend.
'Does he bite?' they said.
'He doesn't bite me,'
I said.
'What's his name?'
they said.
'He doesn't
have one.'

We kept him quiet all day
feeding him our lunches. He liked
the peanut butter sandwiches best.

After school my friends came to the house.

'Where is he?' they said.

We played with the bear
behind the garage.

We made a
tunnel…

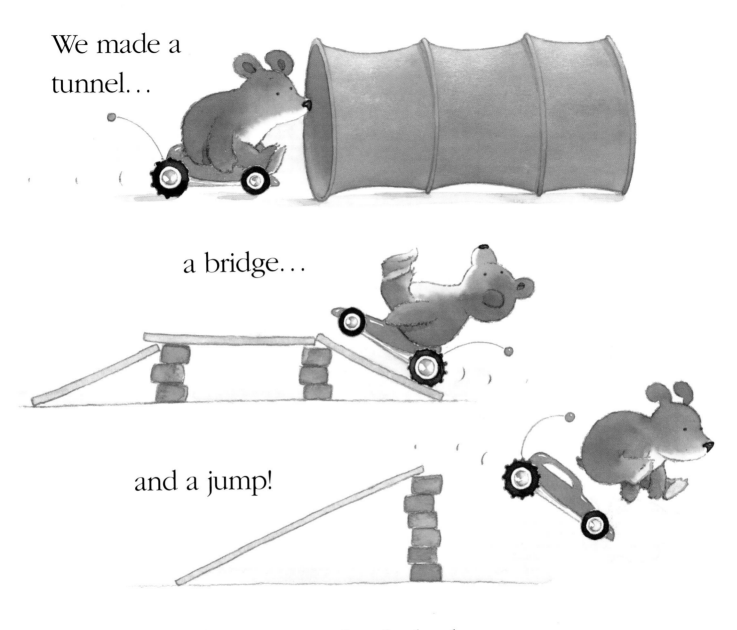

a bridge…

and a jump!

When the car came back the bear
had gone. We looked and looked
but there was no bear anywhere.

At bedtime Sophie
wouldn't go to sleep.

She didn't want her elephant.
She didn't want her rabbit.
She threw them out of the cot.

I gave her my second best pig.
She threw it out.

'Sophie! That's naughty!'
said mum.

But Sophie just howled.
She wanted the bear.

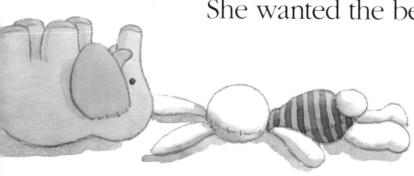

CRASH! BANG!
It was the middle
of the night.
SMASH! CLANG!
The noise was coming from
the kitchen. We crept downstairs
and peeped through the door.
It wasn't a burglar.

'Bear!' said Sophie. 'Naughty!'

So today a serious man in a serious hat came to look at our bear. He wrote something in a big black book.

'Will you have to take him away?' I said.

'We nearly always do,' said the man. He pointed his pen at my bear. 'But,' he said, 'this bear is an Exception.'

'This bear,' he went on, 'has fallen quite unexpectedly into a storybook. And it is not up to me to say what should happen next.'

'So can we keep him?' I said.

'Ask them,' he said. And he
pointed straight out of the picture
at YOU!

And you thought for a moment.
You looked at the man.
You looked at the bear.
You looked at Sophie.
You looked at me.

And then you said…

'YES YOU CAN!'

So we did.

First published 1997
by Hodder Children's Books,
a division of Hodder Headline plc,
338 Euston Road, London NW1 3BH

Paperback edition first published 1998

10 9 8 7 6 5 4 3 2 1

ISBN 0 340 69829 2 (HB)
ISBN 0 340 69830 6 (PB)

A catalogue record for this book
is available from the British Library.
The right of Mick Inkpen to be identified
as the author of this work
has been asserted by him.

Printed in China